Gardening
WITH THE EXPERTS
HERBS

Gardening WITH THE EXPERTS

HERBS

ROSA VALLANCE

HARLAXTON
PUBLISHING

Photographs: Mary Moody: front cover, pages 6, 11, 14.
Manuel Patty: pages 7, 9, 13, 15, 16 (above and below right), 19, 21 (above), 26,27, (below left), 31, 34, 36.
Weldon Trannies: opposite title page, pages 8, 12, 16 (below left), 17, 18, 20, 21 (below),
22, 23, 24-25, 27,(above and below right), 28, 29, 30, 32.

Published by Harlaxton Publishing Ltd
2 Avenue Road, Grantham, Lincolnshire, NG31 6TA, United Kingdom.
A Member of the Weldon International Group of Companies.

First published in 1990 (Limp)
Reprint 1991 (Cased)
Reprint 1992 (Cased)
Reprinted 1993

© Copyright Harlaxton Publishing Ltd
© Copyright design Harlaxton Publishing Ltd

Publishing Manager: Robin Burgess
Illustrations: Kathie Baxter Smith
Typeset in UK by Seller's, Grantham
Produced in Singapore by Imago

British Library Cataloguing-in-Publication data.
A catalogue record for this book is available from the British Library.
Title: Gardening with the Experts: Herbs.
ISBN:1 85837 029 9

CONTENTS

INTRODUCTION 6

HOW TO GROW HERBS: THE BASICS 9

PROPAGATION AND PLANTING 11

WHERE TO PLANT HERBS 19

HERBS FOR VARIOUS PURPOSES 26

CONTAINER HERBS 30

HERBAL FERTILISERS 33

HERBAL INSECTICIDES 34

THE HARVEST 35

IDENTIFICATION AND PLANTING GUIDE 38

INDEX 47

INTRODUCTION

The word 'herb' refers to any of that host of plants, both herbaceous and woody, whose leaves, flowers, seeds, roots, bark and other parts we use for decoration, flavour, fragrance, medicine, cosmetics and dyes.

Most herbaceous plants have soft and succulent rather than woody stems, they include many vegetables along with flowers, shrubs, trees, weeds and grasses. The name 'herb' derives from the Latin *herba* which means grass or green crops.

Their practicality and attractiveness make herbs a valuable asset in any garden. Tradition has dictated that herbs be planted as a separate group, either in an informal or formal herb garden or without much imagination alongside edibles in the vegetable garden. But times are changing!

We are now experiencing a 'herban renewal'— a renaissance of interest in herbs because of our awareness of natural and healthy foods and creative cooking, as well as a resurgence of nostalgia.

Most people, after discovering the pleasure and economy of home-grown produce, start out with a few basic herbs and are soon eager to try others. Nurseries are responding to this interest with a larger selection of new varieties and with more of the old species.

Today, herbs are putting in appearances as part of the total garden landscape. They are happily visible alongside bulbs, annuals, perennials and shrubs. Other ways that herbs can be incorporated into the overall garden picture are as borders or edging around flower beds; among annuals and perennials in blooming borders; as fillers for corners and empty pockets between

A herb garden.

6

Lavender in a garden bed.

other plants; and as ground covers or fragrant carpeting.

Herbs combine well with plants that are usually grown in rock gardens, they thrive on hillsides and slopes or cascading over terraces. You can use them to subdue brilliant colours, selecting grey or silver-foliage species and tucking them alongside other plants so long as their cultivation is compatible.

Then there are container-grown herbs to move about at will, baskets or hanging pots to suspend from roof overhangs, tree branches, fences or walls.

Herbs can be grown in very small spaces. Plant creeping herbs between paving stones; remove a few bricks from a walkway and soften the area with creeping, fragrant herbs; or half-bury hollow cement blocks, then fill them with plants to add interest to an open area.

There is no need to think of herbs as weedy garden plants or a few straggly plants in pots on the kitchen window-sill.

HOW TO GROW HERBS:
THE BASICS

The three requirements for successfully growing herbs as well as many other plants are: light, food and good drainage.

In spite of all the lore surrounding the use of herbs, growing them is no more difficult than growing ordinary flowers or vegetables. Think of them as part of the vegetable garden. Most plants classed as herbs are hardy, easy to grow, practically immune to diseases and pests, adaptable to many types of soil and growing conditions, and quite tolerant of drought and neglect.

Like any group of plants, your attention to their simple wants and needs will be amply rewarded. Most herbs need sunlight for at least five hours a day. Some are tolerant to partial shade and some woodland natives enjoy full shade. Check the requirements of individual plants in the section on "Where to Plant Herbs".

Page opposite: Herbs in a decorative pot.   *Above:* **Sorrel** *prefers well-mulched soil.*

IMPROVING DRAINAGE

In heavy soils, mix coarse grit or sand into the top 45 centimetres. Add compost for fibre to increase bacterial activity. This will make more plant nutrients available. It will also attract earthworm activity which will lighten and further enrich the soil.

Most herbs, like vegetables, prefer a slightly alkaline soil. A light sprinkling of lime or wood ash will help to tone down an acidic soil. Avoid using artificial fertilisers as these can make growth too lush, that eventually results in poor flavour and often reduce the amounts of fragrant oils stored in the leaves.

If your soil is poor you might like to try the some of the suggestions in the "Herbal Fertilisers" section.

Should your soil be very waterlogged or prone to becoming waterlogged, a raised bed might be a permanent solution. These are traditional in herb gardening and also defines areas, allow access for weeding or harvesting and permit access for the infirm in wheelchairs.

PREPARING THE SOIL

Many herbs will survive on poor, stony ground, but they generally prefer a light, slightly sandy soil with good drainage.

In a new bed, prepare the soil in early spring before sowing or planting. Dig deeply, then over several weeks remove persistent weeds and those with taproots. Create a fine tilth, then rake it to a level surface. Let the soil settle for atleast a week before planting seed. However, pot-grown herbs can be planted immediately.

MULCHING

Once herbs are established, mulching will help to prevent soil drying out too quickly and will provide nutrients, especially helpful during the plants' growing season.

A covering of organic matter such as pea straw, rotted hay or bark chip, spread over the soil and around plants, will control weed growth, keep the soil at a cooler and more even temperature as well as visually enhance the plant setting.

Plastic sheeting will tend to make the soil's surface retain too much moisture, it does not allow air circulation, so the soil quickly sours.

If the soil is very moist, those herbs that prefer drier positions, such as mallows or evening primrose, might be happier with a surround of gravel rather than mulch.

PROPAGATION AND PLANTING

You should now be holding and supporting the plant and roots. Slip the plant into the hole, making sure that the soil will come to the same level on the stem as it was in the container, that the soil level is the same as the surrounding soil. Add a little more soil and firm it down gently to eliminate air

Seed and plantlets of common herbs are available at garden centres, nurseries and plant shops, herb societies, herb-growing friends and mail order catalogues .

An enormous number of herbs, both common and rare, can be grown from seed, but if you require only one or two plants it is often more economical and certainly quicker to buy them. When you wish to pop your store-bought or given treasure into the garden, water the soil well beforehand or let the herb soak in a bucket of water for half an hour or so to ensure that the soil and root system hold together.

Make a hole in the soil large enough for the plant's roots. Now turn the pot upside down, with a finger on each side of the stem and touching the soil, give the edge of the pot a sharp rap on the side of a bench.

Parsley seeds should be sown in situ.

pockets. Water the firmed soil to help your new plant settle in. If you know the name of the herb, insert a label into the soil.

For a head start on the growing season or if it is rare or expensive seed, seedlings may be grown indoors. This way, all conditions can be controlled. It is not advisable to start plants with long taproots, such as parsley, indoors unless they are grown in separate large containers, and even then they do not transplant easily.

Use a proprietary loamless, seed-growing mix or mix your own using:

2 parts sterilised and sieved loam
1 part peat or leaf mould
1 part coarse sand
20 grams lime

Blend well and pass through an 8mm sieve. A shallow seed tray (5cm deep) or any flat, clean container that has good drainage may be used for small seed. With small sowings use small pots for economy of soil and space. If using deeper containers, first fill with clean drainage material such as gravel or broken crock. Add growing mix to within 10mm of the top.

Give the tray or pot a sharp downward tap. Then press the soil surface gently with a flat board. If the mix is very dry, water and leave it to drain.

Sow seed thinly, mixing fine seed with a bit of sand for even distribution. Sprinkle a fine layer of potting mix over the seed.

Larger seeds should be covered with a layer as deep as the seed width. In both cases, press the soil down gently and level it if necessary. Carefully and lightly mist the soil with water and date the planting. Cover the container with glass or plastic, or enclose it in a large plastic bag.

It should not be necessary to water again until sprouting begins, but open the cover

A variety of herbs can be grown together in a container.

12

every day for about an hour to let in fresh air and prevent moisture build-up. If dry spots appear on the soil before sprouting commences, set the containers in water (rather than watering them from above which will probably flush the seedlings out of the soil) until the soil is damp.

When sprouting begins, take the cover off and place the container in indirect light for several days. When the first pair of true leaves has formed, after the cotyledons (the two seed leaves which initially emerge), thin the plantlets out or transplant them to a larger pot to prevent overcrowding.

Fill the new container with prepared seedling mix. Handle the transplants by their leaves to prevent bruising or breaking the tiny roots and stems. Using a 'dibbler' or pencil, make a small hole in the soil of the new container and set in the seedling so its leaves are 5cm above the surface. Firm down the soil and water lightly. Set the pot in indirect sunlight.

When the seedlings have grown, remove any weaker subjects, leaving the strongest to continue growing. This will secure the best of the species. The herbs can now be planted in larger pots or out in the garden if there is no danger of frosts.

To avoid shock when planting out, try to pick a calm, warm day, avoiding hot, windy or rainy days. Cloches or light shelter are recommended for the early growing stages outdoors in order to protect the plants from winds, unexpected frost and birds.

SOWING OUTDOORS

Annuals are best sown where you wish them to grow, as root disturbance through transplanting can make them bolt to seed.

Germination depends on three requirements: water, air and warmth. Generally, seed is sown mid to late spring after the soil

Foeniculum vulgare (fennel)

has warmed, or in early autumn.

For spring sowing, new weed seedlings appearing in the garden are a good indication that the time is right for your sowing. Remove the weeds and sow the seed thinly either in shallow drills or freshly prepared beds. Scatter the seed evenly (if very fine, mix it with sand for better distribution) over the area.

Cover the seed thinly with soil and tap it down gently. Water with a fine spray. Label your beds as soon as you have planted them so you will know what is growing where. (Dill and fennel look very similar early on.) Keep the soil moist but never soggy.

Normally annuals take two weeks and perennials about three to four weeks to germinate. Parsley is notoriously slow, taking at least six weeks for germination, so be patient.

For a continuous harvest of short-cycle

herbs such as coriander and borage, make successive sowings several weeks apart. You will sometimes find that seed sown at the same time comes up in batches at various spots. This is a natural protective mechanism for survival of the species and is particularly noticeable in some wild herbs. These herbs will grow only at certain times of the year.

PROPAGATION FROM CUTTINGS, DIVISION AND LAYERING

Cuttings are the most certain way to get plants similar in flower colour and leaf shape to the parent plant. The parent plant gets a beneficial trim in the process. This method is often faster than germination from seed. It is also the most inexpensive and rewarding way to expand your herb collection. Keen herb growers are generally happy to give or exchange cuttings with other growers.

You will need a source of plants, secateurs or a sharp knife, a clear plastic bag, damp paper towelling or something similar to keep cut ends moist (prevent wilting), coarse sand, pumice, peat or propagation mix, pots or deep seed trays.

The three types of cuttings follow the same method of propagation.

Softwood or tip cuttings are taken from non-woody plants. Choose strong new shoots without flower buds.

When taking tip cuttings, cut straight across a shoot so that it is 5 to 10cm in length, with four or five leaf joints. Trim the stem back to just beneath a leaf joint.

Softwood cuttings can be taken most of the year, especially in late spring or after flowering, but not in winter.

Try artemisias or balm, basil, mint, sage, thyme or hyssop.

Semi-hardwood and hardwood cuttings are taken from woody shrubs and trees.

Curry plant, rosemary, rue, santolina, French tarragon and winter savory fall into this category.

With semi-hardwood cuttings, cut pieces 10 to 15cm in length, with hardwoods, 15 to 40cm long. Trim these just below the lowest leaf bud. Hardwood cuttings can be taken from herbs such as lemon verbena from mid to late autumn.

Heel cuttings are taken from shrubby herbs such as rosemary, sage and lavender.

Use a new branch that is starting to firm at the base where it joins the main stem. Pull the branch with a downward movement so that the heel of the older wood of

Mint

the main stem is attached. Using secateurs or a sharp knife, trim the heel, leaving a neat sliver of older wood across the base.

Take heel cuttings from mid-summer to mid-autumn.

For all methods, strip the leaves from the lower third of the cutting before planting, take care not to tear the stem.

If planting outside, choose a warm and sheltered spot, if possible out of direct sunlight. Firmly plant the cutting with the cut side down in gritty or peaty soil, keep it moist. An ideal spot might be under the mother plant.

With container planting, place a third of the length of the cuttings in the potting medium, either singly or with several around the edge of the pot, water, then

PROPAGATION FROM CUTTINGS

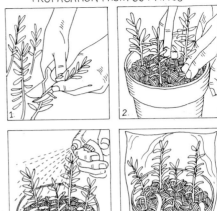

1. TAKE CUTTINGS WITH SHARP SECATEURS. 2. INSERT CUTTINGS INTO CLEAN POTS. 3. WATER THOROUGHLY. 4. ENCLOSE POTS IN CLEAR PLASTIC UNTIL ROOTED.

Basil

cover them with a plastic bag raised above the leaves to prevent mildew.

This will provide the cuttings with the moisture and warmth that will speed up the rooting process. Open the bag every few days to allow fresh air to enter and to prevent mould build-up.

When the foliage seems to perk up, the bag may be removed. As soon as signs of new growth are noticed (this may be one month for tender-stemmed herbs such as sage, to several months for woody stemmed varieties), transfer the plants to containers and place these in a sheltered spot with indirect sunlight, gradually increasing exposure to direct sunlight over a period of two weeks. Apply weak liquid fertiliser or compost for plant nutrients.

Hardwood cuttings will develop over the winter and ought to be ready for spring planting. If a plant's roots show at the base of the container, transplant it to a larger pot or plant it in a permanent position.

15

Root Cutting propagation of Lemon balm, sage, rosemary and comfrey can be carried out in spring and autumn.

Dig up the plant and remove pieces of root 5cm in diameter that have bud growth. Cut these pieces into 5cm long sections and discard the thin ends.

Place these vertically into moistened potting mix in a container and cover with 5cm of sand. Cover with a plastic bag and follow the procedure for tip cuttings until there are signs of growth.

When the plants have gained substantial growth, they can be repotted or planted out in the garden,

Root Division is a simple method of severing the roots so that some top growth remains attached to each piece.

This is usually done with plants that grow in clumps, such as costmary, yarrow, mint, lemon balm, lady's bedstraw and

Sage

Rosemary

Bergamot

bergamot. Division checks the spread of these herbs and keeps them hardier, besides giving the keen gardener multiple plants for replanting or giving away.

Division is best attempted either in spring, before there is much new growth, or in autumn, after plants become dormant.

Simply wet the soil around the plant, dig it up or take it out of its pot, separate the plant into sections by pulling it apart with your fingers or with two forks back to back, or by cutting through sections with a spade or secateurs.

Make sure each section has a growing point and some roots. Discard hard old growth and tidy up the plant as you go.

Replant the sections in the ground or in containers. Keep the soil moist until the plants adjust to their new situations.

Layering is pegging down or covering with soil, part of a stem from the mother plant. Many plants, such as thyme will often do this naturally.

Bend a stem that will touch the earth just below a leaf node about 10cm from the growing tip. Peg it to the ground with bent wire or a short, forked branch so that contact is made with the soil. Keep this area moist. Check for root development in six weeks.

When roots are established, cut the stem from the parent just above the new roots. Dig up the roots and stem then plant them in a container or directly in the garden.

If you attempt this in autumn and your region experiences frosts, cover the contact point with mulch to prevent damage from unexpected frosts.

A clump of pennyroyal seedlings being separated by root division.

Thyme

Mound Layering of plants such as sage and thyme, which can become woody in the centre, can be improved in appearance or propagated in spring by mounding soil over the woody centre until only young growth shows.

Check in eight weeks for new roots at the base of the shoots. When the roots are established, cut the rooted shoot from the parent plant and proceed as for layering.

Lemon balm

WHERE TO PLANT HERBS

HERBS FOR DRY GROUND

Dry ground, walls and earthen banks are ideal environments for most culinary and aromatic herbs as many originate fromthe Mediterranean, often in harsh scrub land.

The volatile oils and flavours are a product of the sun and set by warm winds. These herbs have developed colours and tough leaves to conserve moisture which otherwise, the winds would draw out and

the sun would evaporate. To repel browsing animals, the plants have developed spiky tips, leathery surfaces and volatile oils which form a protective vapour around the plant. These characteristics together with their pungent flavours ensure some survival from herbivores.

To imitate their natural environment, a stony, well-drained garden bed, a sunny position and a not-too-rich soil is ideal.

Tropaeolum majus (Nasturtiums) thrive in rockeries or in the crevices of walls.

Lavender growing on top of a wall.

For walls or rockeries, any herb with 'wall' in its name is an obvious choice, such as wall germander or wallflower.

Others you might like to try in crevices or on top of a sunny wall are nasturtiums, perennial chamomile, and any prostrate form of catmint, rosemary, sage or savory. For the very top of a wall, hyssop, santolina and lavender are very suitable.

For really dry corners where the soil is poor and thin, only the most tolerant and toughest of herbs, bugloss*, mugwort, species of mallow, mullein, yarrow, evening primrose or white horehound will survive.

Other herbs suitable for dry environments are artemisias, curry plant, costmary, fennel, lady's bedstraw, hypericum*, musk mallow, marjorams, weld, rue, meadow clary, salad burnet, betony, feverfew, tansy and vervain.

HERBS FOR SHADY PLACES
Many woodland herbs will grow well in the shade of a wall or beneath a tree.

Generally, these will be perennials that flower early and continue to have interesting foliage, a bonus when spring flowering is over. This is an important consideration for your overall garden plan.

For heavy shade: bugle, woodruff, pennyroyal, evening primrose, lungwort valerian and sweet violet.

For partial shade: lady's mantle, angelica, foxglove, wild strawberry, ground ivy, sweet cicely, wood sage and orris.

For light shade: chives, marshmallow, chervil, foxglove, rocket, meadowsweet, lady's bedstraw, hypericum, musk mallow, lemon balm, the mints, the parsleys and comfrey.

* These herbs are considered noxious weeds in some regions. Please check with your local authority before planting them.

Sweet marjoram (above) and salad burnet (below).

HERBS FOR WATERY SURROUNDS AND DAMP GROUND

Very few herbs need a really muddy place in the garden. A reasonably water retentive soil is usually sufficient.

These herbs will tolerate light or dappled shade. Most have medicinal or household uses and they are generally perennials. Unlike woodland plants, they will begin to blossom from early summer onwards.

Comfrey and elecampane will survive in a patch of heavy, damp soil if nothing else seems to grow. These are the most tolerant of herbs, growing in spreading clumps to large-sized plants. For fragrant flowers in early summer, valerian, agrimony and meadowsweet do admirably. Sweet cicely, with its soft green, fernlike leaves, will put on a delicate show of white flowers in early spring in a damp spot or beneath a tree.

Other herbs for damp spots are angelica, sneezewort, marshmallow and soapwort .

Above: A lightly shaded area is suitable for peppermint.
*Page opposite: Foxgloves (**digitalis**) prefer partial or light shade.*

HERBS FOR VARIOUS PURPOSES

SCENT

Scented flowers: These include evening primrose, lady's bedstraw, lavenders, lemon verbena, meadowsweet, mignonette, sages, rocket, chives, bergamot, calendula, chamomile, mallow and valerian, some with delicate scents and some with powerful smells.

Scents are very personal preferences, and what one individual finds pleasant another may find abhorrent.

Check with your nose when buying herbs.

Scented foliage: These herbs are lovely when planted where they will be brushed against. They will release their fragrance when they are touched or picked:

Agrimony, angelica, artemisias, anise, anise hyssop, balm of Gilead, basils, sweet bay, bergamot, camphor, caraway, catmint, chamomile, chervil, coriander, costmary, dill, fennel, lavenders, lemon balm, lemon grass, lemon verbena, lovage, marjorams, oregano, pyrethrum, rosemary, rue, sages,

Evening primrose produces scented flowers.

Anise has fragrant foliage

santolina, savories, sweet cicely, tansy, thymes, tarragon, curry and motherwort, to name but some.

To entice bees: These herbs planted in full sun will ensure a long flowering period and a steady stream of busy, workers—anise hyssop, balm of Gilead, bergamot, betony, borage, caraway, catmint, catnip, hyssop, lavenders, lemon balm, lungwort, marjoram, mignonette, rosemary, sages, savories and thymes.

To repel insects: The following do an

Oregano leaves are strongly scented.

Bees are attracted to the caraway plant.

admirable job in the garden and home—artemisias, basils, chives, feverfew, garlic, mint, pyrethrum, rue, santolina, tansy.

EDGES, HEDGES, LAWNS AND GROUND COVERS

For edges: Alpine strawberry, basils, chives, wall germander, dwarf lavenders, marjorams, parsleys, dwarf rosemary, rue, sages, salad burnet, savories, thyme, violets.

For hedges: Sweet bay, common sage, curry plant, hyssop, lavenders, rosemary.

For lawns: Lawn chamomile, pennyroyal and the smaller thymes.

For ground covers: Bugle, chamomile, ground ivy, lady's bedstraw, Corsican mint, nasturtiums, oregano, pennyroyal, prostrate rosemary, prostrate winter savory, sweet woodruff and wild thymes.

FOLIAGE COLOUR

Silver or grey leaves: Use these to lighten a dark corner, to contrast with darker colours or to break up a colour scheme. They are very effective in mass plantings. The artemisias, camphor, catmint, clary sage, costmary, curry plant, white horehound, lavenders, mullein, pyrethrum, rue, common sage, santolina, and orange and woolly thyme.

Darker leaves: With red leaves — purple basil, bronze fennel, red sage; with green leaves — anthemis (dyer's chamomile), wall germander, ground ivy, meadowsweet, rosemary, some thymes.

Yellow or orange leaves: Aureum marjoram, aureum feverfew and some varieties of thyme.

The colour of Yarrow flowers varies with the species.

FLOWER COLOUR

White or cream: Anise, applemint, basil, borage, caraway, curry plant, lemon balm, garlic chives, Roman chamomile, meadowsweet, woodruff, orris, musk mallow, sweet marjoram, sweet cicely, Welsh comfrey, feverfew, winter savory and some yarrows.

Yellow or orange: Agrimony, calendula, dyer's chamomile, chamomile, lady's bedstraw, curry plant, feverfew, hypericum, elecampane, evening primrose, santolina, nasturtiums, tansy, mullein, woad, yarrow.

Blue or mauve: Anise hyssop, betony, borage, bugle, catmint, chives, hyssop, most lavenders, lungwort, some mints, orris, rosemary, sage, some thymes, violets.

Pink or red: Balm of Gilead, some basils, bergamot, betony, comfrey, coriander, lungwort, marshmallow, musk mallow, golden marjoram, motherwort, pineapple sage, red sage, summer savory, soapwort, some thymes, valerian and red yarrow.

Green-yellow: Lady's mantle, dill, fennel, lady's bedstraw, lovage, weld, rue.

HEIGHT

As the height of plants can determine the focal point of a garden, the eye is led to distances, to mark corners, note steps or seats, or windbreaks where they are needed or provided.

The following list gives plants in order of height (with the tallest first):

Evergreen trees and shrubs: Sweet bay 7m, box 3m, rosemary 2.5m, lavender 1.2m

The evergreen shrub southernwood is often grown in cottage gardens.

apothecary rose 1.2m, Jerusalem sage 1.2m, wormwood 1m, southernwood 90cm, santolina 80cm, sage 75cm, curry plant 60cm.

Perennial herbs: Elecampane 2m, lovage 2m, sweet cicely 1.5m, valerian 1.5m, comfrey 1.5m, mugwort 1.5m, tansy 1.5m, catnip 1.5m, meadowsweet 1m, fennel 1m, marshmallow 1m, vervain 1m.

Biennial herbs: Angelica 2m, mullein 2m, weld 1.5m, clary sage 1.2m, evening primrose 1m.

Annual herb: Dill 1.5m.

CONTAINER HERBS

There are times when, through preference, for ease of access, for confinement, for a plant's survival or because of lack of garden space, container planting really comes into its own. You can prolong the growing season of herbs, place them where they can appeal to your sense of smell, and create a visually appealing environment which is a constant source of interest.

Pots of herbs look attractive when grouped.

Although herbs thrive more vigorously in the ground, with a certain amount of care and commonsense you can grow them in pots, either indoors or outdoors.

When placing containers on balconies or freestanding structures, take care that these can support the weighty combination of soil and water. Exposure to the wind must also be considered. Small containers may be blown over and tender-leaved herbs can be quickly damaged by strong winds.

Herbs in a group of pots can provide a focal point and look more pleasing to the eye than one lonely specimen. They seem to enjoy each other's company and benefit from the microclimate that grouping creates. By changing the position of the pots, you can fill seasonal gaps or vary the appearance of your garden. Herbs in pots are an excellent way to create different colour schemes in small or large areas. A silver or moonlight garden would have artemisias, santolinas and curry plants; a golden garden would have lemon thyme, variegated sage, variegated lemon balm, calendula, lady's bedstraw and nasturtiums; a blue garden would have hyssop, borage, catmint, rosemary and sage.

The space needed by particular plants will dictate how many can be put in a planter. A metre-long container can hold four or five low-growing herbs, such as sage, thyme, marjoram and salad burnet,

which will benefit from being kept well trimmed. A delightful addition to a barbecue area is a tub or barrel filled with culinary herbs such as rosemary, chives, sage, mint (in its own container) or lemon balm, to add colour and fragrance to outdoor entertaining.

Remember, these plants are dependent

A wall planter with violets

on your care and more vulnerable than plants in the open ground. Some general rules for successful container planting are as follows:

1. Always start with a clean pot. Wash the pot with hot water and washing soda or soap, or with a weak solution of household bleach, rinsing well.
2. Provide the plants with good drainage. For seedlings, add some coarse pumice to the bottom of the pot.
3. Make sure that the soil is friable and porous. Do not use ordinary garden soil. A good commercial potting mix is suitable for older plants but is often too rich for tiny seedlings. Traditional potting compound can be made by combining 7 parts loam, 3 parts peat and 2 parts gritty or sharp sand with some well-rotted compost. Do not use builder's sand since it will become compact, making drainage worse. Keep the mixture loose and open to prevent fungal spore formation.
4. Ensure that the sizes of the container and the plant are compatible. Small plants flounder in large pots.
5. Check regularly for aphids and thrips and deal with these pests if infestation is present. See the "Herbal Insecticides" section in this book.
6. Monitor indoor herbs regularly for their need for watering. Do not water them unnecessarily but never allow them to become bone dry. Rosemary never fully recovers if it dries out totally, yet sage will collapse if watered too frequently. Overwatering can cause rootrot by eliminating vital air pockets, needed by root hairs. An occasional spray with tepid water from a mister is useful in hot weather for soft-leaved herbs such as basil.

7. Remove deadheads, trim the leaves back and keep the pot weed-free to aid vigorous growth.

8. Feed herbs through their leaves or the soil every two weeks during the growing season, easing off as the growth rate slows and stop altogether during the dormant period.

9. Meet the herbs' light requirements but do not let the pots get too hot.

10. If a herb looks sad, check if it needs water, less water or food, whether it is sitting in a draught or whether it is receiving the correct amount of light.

Mint should be grown in its own container.

HERBAL FERTILISERS

Comfrey: One comfrey plant will provide four crops a year. Comfrey fertiliser supplies nitrogen, phosphorus, potash and trace elements. Method: Pick the leaves from late spring to midsummer. Let them wilt for at least forty-eight hours, mulch them and apply the mulch directly to plants, or soak fresh leaves in water for four weeks and use the liquid as a fertiliser.

Dill: This is rich in potassium, sulphur, sodium and other minerals.

Tansy: Tansy is rich in potassium and other minerals.

Yarrow: This provides copper and is a good general fertiliser.

Basic Recipe: Pour 1 litre of boiling

water over a handful of fresh herbs or over 30 grams of dried herbs, cover, infuse for ten minutes and strain before using.

Do not use aluminium vessels.

HERBAL INSECTICIDES

Basil leaves can be used to repel aphids. For method, see chamomile flowers below.

Costmary leaves can be used as a general insecticide. For method, see chamomile flowers below.

Wormwood leaves should be used only on mature plants (because of its toxicity) against larger pests such as caterpillars, moths, flea beetles and aphids. Method: Put 15 grams of dried herbs in 1 litre of cold water. Simmer covered for half an hour. Turn heat off and steep for fifteen minutes. Do not use aluminium vessels.

Chamomile flowers prevent damping off in seedlings. Method: Pour 1 litre of boiling water over 30 ml of dried flowers or over a handful of fresh flowers. Cover, steep for ten minutes, strain and use at once.

Pyrethrum is a natural insecticide which rapidly paralyses insects. Its flower heads can be dried or powdered and used against all common sucking insects: bedbugs, mosquitoes, cockroaches and domestic fly. Prolonged contact with the flower heads can cause allergic reactions in some people, so rubber gloves are a must. Method: Pick the open flower heads. Dry and pulverise them. To make a spray, steep 30 grams of powder in 50 ml of methylated spirits. Dilute this with 18 litres of water.

Proprietary brands of this insecticide are also available. Spray the insecticide at dusk so that plants and bees will be safe. The solution will have dispersed by morning, especially if exposed to bright sunlight.

Chamomile flowers help to prevent damping-off in seedlings.

THE HARVEST

PICKING AND HARVESTING

After spending time sowing and planting, herb gardeners reap their just rewards.

Most culinary herbs can be used from the seedling stage, as their flavours are already present. Keep in mind that, as you snip and pick, you are determining the future shape of the growing plant. If you harvest leaves judiciously, the plant will become fuller and bushier.

Evergreen herbs, such as sage, thyme, basil, tarragon and marjoram, maintain a bushier shape if the growing tip is pinched out first. In general, do not remove more than a fifth of the herb's leaves in order to allow regeneration and growth of the plant.

When harvesting for preserving ensure that the herbs have not been sprayed recently with pesticides or herbicides. (If they have been sprayed, wait the time recommended by the manufacturer's instructions before harvesting.)

For maximum flavour preservation, harvest leaves in the morning after the dew has evaporated and before the sun has had a chance to bring out the oils. Then, using a flat bottomed basket or box, place the leaves gently on the base in order to avoid bruising them and losing the essential oils, therefore, the flavour.

Pick only the amount you feel you can use in the near future. To simplify harvesting large quantities, it is recommended that you handle only one species at a time, to leave you time to pick over the harvest for badly blemished leaves, then to sort and tie the remainder into bunches, if necessary.

Leaves that will be eaten as salad greens — borage, burnet, nasturtiums, rocket, sorrel and winter savory — should be picked when young, before they flower, when they are at their most succulent.

Grassy-stalked leaves such as chives and parsley should be cut or pulled just above ground level. These salad herbs, which include angelica, are not suitable for drying and can be preserved by other means.

Aromatic evergreens such as rosemary, sage, savory and thyme have maximum flavour just before flowering. Basil, lovage, marjoram and mint have a sweeter flavour just before flowering. Using secateurs to

collect whole stems of these small-leaved herbs speeds up collection and makes drying more convenient.

If you wish to harvest the whole plant, perennials can be cut back to half the length of the year's growth; annuals can be cut to about 8 cm above the ground at the first harvest (early summer) and in autumn, to ground level.

Seed heads are ready for harvesting when they have lost their green colour and feel dry to the touch, preferably before they have scattered their seeds on the ground.

The seeds should be collected on a dry, warm day. Shake small seeds directly into a paper bag, or pop the heads or stems into bags, labelling and dating as you go. Remember to collect annual and culinary seeds for next year's propagation, let some such as dill and fennel self-sow, to ensure a crop next year.

Roots are best harvested in autumn. Annual roots are harvested when their growth cycle is complete, but perennial roots in their second or third year growth, when their active components, such as volatile oils or alkaloids, have developed. After digging up the root, take off what you require and replant the remainder to continue growing.

Most fleshy roots can be scrubbed clean, but others such as valerian should not be as they lose their active constituents.

Flowers are gathered as they fully open, the stalked varieties such as lavenders being snipped whole and the others picked carefully to avoid wilting or damage, especially if you wish to crystallise those such as violets and borage. Once picked, the flowers should be kept loose, not touching, in open containers to prevent sweating and bruising. Calendula petals are removed from the flowers to be dried and

stored, while other small-headed flowers such as chamomile are dried intact.

PRESERVING THE HARVEST

Leaves and flowers may now be dried in a variety of ways — by hanging them upside down in bunches in a warm, dry, dark area with some air movement, or by placing them on cloth frames or wire racks in such an area.

Dry strongly flavoured herbs such as lovage separately, away from other herbs, so that their flavours do not mingle. A loft, a sheltered garage ceiling or a hot water cupboard are all suitable places. If the drying area is dusty or if you are drying stems with seed heads, cover the bunches with brown paper bags loosely tied. These will act as dust covers and will catch seeds as they fall off stems or out of capsules.

Drying takes anywhere from five days to two weeks. Then your harvest is ready, it should be crisp and papery to the touch. A quicker method is to spread leaves on a muslin-covered rack in an oven which is set at a low temperature with the door open to let moisture escape.

Turn and stir the herbs until crisp. Small

quantities can be processed in a microwave oven, but although the flavour may not be affected, the therapeutic properties, such as those in chamomile, may be destroyed.

Roots should be cleaned, with fibrous parts removed, and cut into small, even portions or segments. Dry these in the oven at 120 to 140°C, turning them at intervals until they feel fragile and can be easily broken.

Leaves should be removed from stems and stored in labelled airtight, glass or plastic containers away from light, heat, moisture and contamination. Check them periodically for damp, mould and insects

and discard them if these conditions occur. When properly dried, stored herbs will retain their freshness and flavour for at least a year.

Flowers, that have been dried the same way as leaves, are best stored spread out so that they maintain their shape, especially fragile flowers such as borage and violets.

Seeds for culinary use should be labelled and stored as leaves are, and seed for sowing should be kept in a cool, dark place free from frost.

Roots should also stored in airtight containers in a dark place. Those such as angelica and parsley may re-absorb air moisture. If this occurs and they become soft, discard them.

Other methods of preserving herbs include freezing, packing in vinegar or oil, and salt curing.

One of the most satisfying rewards for the herb grower is to present a friend, family member or neighbour with a generous bunch of fragrant, beautiful herbs, with the knowledge that they were carefully grown, tended and harvested by your own hand.

IDENTIFICATION AND PLANTING GUIDE

Abbreviations: A Annual; B Biennial; P Perennial; HP Herbaceous Perennial; WP Woody Perennial; Sp Spring; S Summer; A Autumn; W Winter; E Early; L Late

Herb	Habit	Propagation	Spacing	Comments
Agrimony (*Agrimonia eupatoria*)	P. Upright, compact, grows to 60 cm.	Seed—Sp Division—Sp and A	40 cm	Self-sows readily. Can become weedlike, but beautiful apricot scent.
All herb (*Coleus amboinicus*)	A. Fleshy leaves, thick stems. Sprawling plant, grows to 1 m.	Seed—Sp Cuttings—Sp	30 cm	Tropical plant, annual in temperate climate. Attractive pot plant.
Alpine strawberry (*Fragaria alpina*)	P. Clump-forming, compact, grows to 30 cm.	Seed—Sp and S Division—A	20 cm	Grows well in hanging baskets. Delicious strawberry fruit.
Angelica (*Angelica archangelica*)	B. Large leaves at base, flowering stalk, 2nd year grows to 1.5 m.	Fresh seed—A	1 m	Large but compact. Whole plant aromatic.
Anise (*Pimpinella anisum*)	A. Slender plant, grows to 50 cm.	Seed—Sp	20 cm	Long warm period needed to flower and set seed.
Anise hyssop (*Agastache foeniculum*)	P. Tall main stem, compact and upright, grows to 1 m.	Seed—Sp and A Cuttings—EA	30 cm	Short-lived bee plant. Long-lasting flowers.
Artemisia mugwort (*A. vulgaris*)	HP. Clump spreading to 1 m.	Seed—Sp Division—Sp	50 cm	Pungent and balsamic. Self-sows readily. Can become invasive.
Roman wormwood (*A. pontica*)	HP. Spreading clump, grows to 40 cm. Dies down in winter.	Division—Sp and A	40 cm	Deeply divided, grey, aromatic leaves. Keep trimmed.

38

Herb	Habit	Propagation	Spacing	Comments
tree wormwood (*A. arborescens*)	WP. Compact, large bush, grows to 80 cm.	Cuttings—Sp and A	80 cm	Good coastal hedge. Cut back S and A.
wormwood (*A. absinthum*)	HP. Upright, spreading, fernlike plant, grows to 1.5 m.	Seed—Sp Division—Sp and A	40 cm	Will keep animals from the garden. Cut after flowering.
Balm of Gilead (*Cedronella canariensis*)	WP. Camphor-scented, sprawling shrub, grows to 1 m.	Seed—Sp Cuttings—Sp and A	80 cm	Good bee plant. Prune regularly.
Basil				
bush basil (*O. minimum*)	A. Bright green bush, grows to 20 cm.	Seed—Sp	20 cm	As for sweet basil. Good container plant.
lettuce-leaf basil (*O. crispum*)	A. Crinkled, bright green, large leaves, grows to 50 cm.	Seed—Sp	40 cm	Needs protection from cold when young.
perennial basil (*Ocimum* spp.)	P. Green, compact bush, grows to 50 cm.	Seed—Sp	40 cm	Will not tolerate frosts or cold damp.
purple basil (*O. basilicum purpurescens*)	A. Similar to sweet basil but purple-leaved, grows to 50 cm.	Seed—Sp	30 cm	Needs protection from cold when young.
sacred basil (*O. sanctum*)	A. Soft, hairy, compact bush, grows to 30 cm.	Seed—Sp	30 cm	Needs protection from cold when young.
sweet basil (*Ocimum basilicum*)	A. Bright green bush, grows to 50 cm.	Seed—Sp	30 cm	Needs protection from cold, especially when young.
Bay (*Laurus nobilis*)	Compact shrub or tree, grows to 20 m when mature.	Seed—Sp Cuttings—Sp and A	1 m	Slow-growing. Good pot or lawn specimen or pruned as hedge.
Bergamot (*Monarda didyma*)	HP. Spreading clump with flowers. Grows to 60 cm.	Seed—Sp Division—Sp and A	40 cm	Needs protection from frost. Cut back in A. Good bee plant.

Herb	Habit	Propagation	Spacing	Comments
Betony (*Stachys officinalis*)	P. Compact clump with flowers, grows to 60 cm.	Seed—Sp Division—Sp and A	40 cm	Likes semi-shade. Cut off old growth. Flowers S and A.
Borage (*Borago officinalis*)	A. Most tolerant plant, grows to 1 m.	Seed—Sp and A	1 m	Bees love its blue flowers. Self-sows freely.
Bugle (*Ajuga reptans*)	P. Low-spreading, tolerant plant with flowers, grows to 15 cm.	Seed—Sp Division—Sp and A	20 cm	Grows well in pots. Good ground cover and rockery plant.
Calendula (pot marigold— *C. officinalis*)	A. Sprawling, bushy habit, grows to 50 cm.	Seed—Sp Division—Sp and A	50 cm	Cut back regularly for constant flowering. Self-sows readily. Will grow in poor soils.
Caraway (*Carum carvi*)	A/B (depends on when seed is sown). Slender plant, grows in clump to 50 cm.	Seed—Sp and A	40 cm	Will rot in winter if drainage is poor. Seeds used in bread making.
Catmint (*Nepeta mussinii*)	P. Low, bushy growth with flowers, grows to 20 cm. Dies down in W.	Seed—Sp Division—Sp and A	50 cm	Ornamental form of catnip. Perfect foil for roses and borders.
Catnip (*Nepeta cataria*)	P. Strong stems grow to 1–2 m. Dies down in winter.	Seed—Sp Division—Sp and A	30 cm	Cats drool over it. Protect young plants.
Chamomile German chamomile (*Matricaria chamomila*)	A. Flowering stems grow to 30 cm.	Seed—Sp and A	15 cm	The dried flowers make excellent tea. Likes sun.
Roman chamomile (*Anthemis nobilis*)	P. Low, spreading plant with trailing stems, grows to 15 cm.	Seed—Sp Division—Sp and A	15 cm	Beautifully scented herb for lawn, seat, path or bank. Prefers sandy soil.

Herb	Habit	Propagation	Spacing	Comments
Chervil (*Anthriscus cerefolium*)	A. Compact, fernlike, bright green plant, grows to 80 cm.	Seed—Sp and A	20 cm	Self-sows readily. Likes cool spots. Good under deciduous trees.
Chives (*Allium schoenoprasum*)	HP. Clumps of shoots from bulbs grow to 20–50 cm. Dies back in winter.	Seed—Sp and S Bulb division—S and A	20 cm	Lift and divide every 2 years. Good edging and pot plant.
garlic chives (*A. tuberosum*)	HP. Less dense clump than chives. Grows to 30–50 cm.	As for chives	20 cm	As for chives.
Comfrey (*Symphytum officinalis*)	P. Vigorous, upright plant, grows to 1.5 m.	Division—Sp	70 cm	Needs to be contained. Plant out in permanent position.
Coriander (*Coriandrum sativum*)	A. Delicate shrublike plant, grows to 50 cm.	Seed—Sp and A	20 cm	Will self-sow. Unusual pungent scent.
Costmary (*Chrysanthemum balsamita*)	P. Sprawling, rooted clump with flowering stem to 1.5 m.	Division—Sp and A	60 cm	Very old cultivar, also known as alecost and bible leaf.
Curry plant (*Helichrysum angustifolium*)	P. Low, silvery bush with flower heads to 20 cm.	Stem cuttings—Sp and A	30 cm	Prune lightly ESp and A. Good edging and border plant.
Dill (*Anethum graveolens*)	A. Tall, feathery plant, grows to 80 cm.	Seed—Sp, S and A	70 cm	Needs some wind protection.
Feverfew (*Chrysanthemum parthenium*)	WP. Bright green, tolerant plant, grows to 70 cm.	Seed—Sp and A Cuttings—Sp Division—Sp	40 cm	Self-sows readily. Cut back after flowering.
Horehound (*Marrubium vulgare*)	HP. Silvery, bushy growth to 50 cm.	Seed—LSp Division—Sp Cuttings—S	30 cm	Some wind protection needed. Prune in Sp to prevent woodiness.
Hyssop (*Hyssopus officinalis*)	WP. Hardy, bushy shrub, grows to 40 cm.	Seed—Sp Cuttings—Sp Division—A	40 cm	Cut back in A. Good low hedge or border plant to attract bees and butterflies.

Herb	Habit	Propagation	Spacing	Comments
Lady's bedstraw (*Galium verum*)	P. Hardy, honey-scented, delicate plant, grows to 15 cm.	Seed—S Division—Sp and A	40 cm	Attractive and useful ground cover. A dyer's plant.
Lavender English lavender (*Lavandula angustifolia*)	WP. Bushy, compact, grey shrub, grows to 80 cm. Dwarf forms available.	Seed—Sp Cuttings—Sp and A	40 cm	Beautiful hedge or specimen. Cut back after flowering.
French lavender (*L. dentata*)	WP. Bushy, compact, grey shrub with toothed leaves. Grows to 1 m.	As for English lavender	60 cm	Good medium-sized hedge plant. Flowers most of the year.
green lavender (*L. viridis*)	WP. Green-foliaged, compact shrub with distinct scent. Grows to 60 cm.	As for English lavender	40 cm	Cut back in A. Soil must be well drained.
Lemon balm (*Melissa officinalis*)	P. Bright green, tolerant shrub, grows in clump to 2 m.	Seed—Sp and A Division—Sp and A	60 cm	Cut back after flowering. Self-sows easily.
Lemon verbena (*Lippia citriodora*)	P. Deciduous shrub, grows to 2.5 m when mature.	Seed—Sp Softwood cuttings—Sp	1 m	Needs some shelter when young and is frost tender.
Lovage (*Levisticum officinale*)	HP. Vigorous, tall stalks to 2 m.	Seed—Sp and A Division—Sp and A	60 cm	A stately, strongly aromatic plant. Good background specimen.
Marjoram golden marjoram (*Origanum majorana*)	WP. Golden, low-creeping bush. May die back in winter.	Seed—Sp Division—Sp and A	30 cm	Striking ground cover. Good in tubs.
pot marjoram (*O. onites*)	HP. Grows to 50 cm. Bushy habit. Dies back in W.	Seed—Sp Division—LSp	40 cm	Hardy form with robust flavour.

Herb	Habit	Propagation	Spacing	Comments
sweet marjoram (*Majorana hortensis*)	WP. Small grey-green bush, grows to 30–50 cm. Grown as annual.	Seed—Sp Cuttings—A Division—A	30 cm	Best form for culinary use.
wild marjoram (*O. vulgare*)	HP. Forms dense mat with flowering stems to 60 cm.	Seed—Sp Division—LSp	40 cm	Often called oregano. The least aromatic of all.
Mint (*Mentha* spp.) applemint (*M. suaveolens*)	HP. Vigorous, spreading clump with soft, green, downy leaves.	Seed—Sp Division—Sp	50 cm	Needs to be contained. Looks good in large pots.
eau de cologne mint (*M. ×piperita* 'Citrata')	P. Wine and green stems. Flowering to 1 m. Dies back in winter.	Division—Sp and S	50 cm	Lovely fresh scent. Can become invasive so needs to be contained.
pennyroyal (*M. pulegium*)	P. A vigorous, spreading clump with flowers, grows to 20–30 cm.	Seed—Sp Division—Sp and A	30 cm	Good ground cover. Can be used for lawn.
peppermint (*M. piperita*)	P. Vigorous, spreading clump flowering to 60 cm. W dormant.	Seed—Sp Division—Sp and S	50 cm	Old culinary favourite. Needs to be contained.
spearmint (*M. spicata*)	HP. Creeping rootstock. Grows to 1 m in flower. Dies down in W.	As for peppermint	30 cm	Best culinary mint.
Parsley (*Petroselinum* spp.) curly-leaf parsley (*P. crispum*)	B. Compact clump, grows to 60 cm. Dark green leaves.	Seed—Sp and A	40 cm	Milder flavour than plain-leaf parsley. Germination takes 4–6 weeks.

Herb	Habit	Propagation	Spacing	Comments
plain-leaf parsley (*P. neopolitanum*)	B. Compact clump, grows to 70 cm. Dark green, divided leaves.	As for curly-leaf parsley	50 cm	Very hardy, strong-flavoured, culinary herb. Self-sows.
Rocket (*Eruca sativa*)	A. Quick-growing salad herb. Grows to 30–70 cm.	Seed—Sp and S	20 cm	Self-sows readily. Harvest young leaves regularly.
Rosemary (*Rosmarinus officinalis*)	WP. Sprawling, woody shrub, grows to 50 cm.	Seed—Sp Cuttings—Sp and A	60 cm	Good hedge plant. Keep trimmed for shape. Prefers limy soil.
prostrate rosemary (*R. prostrata*)	WP. Trailing creeper, grows to 15 cm.	Seed—Sp Cuttings—Sp and A Layering—Sp, S and A	40 cm	Good hardy ground cover. Used in rockeries, hanging containers. Slow to germinate.
Rue (*Ruta graveolens*)	P. Tolerant, pungent, blue-green, compact bush, grows to 1 m.	Seed—Sp Cuttings—Sp and S	50 cm	Prefers dry soil.
Sage (*Salvia officinalis*)	WP. Short-lived, bushy, compact shrub, grows to 80 cm.	Seed—Sp Cuttings—Sp and A Layering—Sp and S	40 cm	Many cultivars with various leaf and flower colours. Broad-leaf does not flower.
clary sage (*S. sclarea*)	B. Tall, sprawling clump, grows to 1 m.	Seed—Sp and A	60 cm	An ornamental that needs lots of space.
pineapple sage (*S. rutilans*)	WP. Stems to 1 m and red flowers all winter.	Cuttings—Sp and A Division—Sp	60 cm	Frost sensitive. Cut back LW. Bees love it.
Salad burnet (*Sanguisorba minor*)	P. Dainty, leafy clump, grows to 20–25 cm. Flowering stalks to 50 cm.	Seed—Sp and A	40 cm	Useful low border plant. Grows well in W.

Herb	Habit	Propagation	Spacing	Comments
Santolina (lavender cotton— *S. chamaecyparissus*)	WP. Coral-like, grey, scented, compact bush, grows to 45 cm.	Seed—Sp Cuttings—Sp and A	30 cm	Trim after flowering. Good low hedge, contrast and rockery plant.
Savory summer savory (*Satureja hortensis*)	A. Green-red, compact bush, grows to 25–40 cm.	Seed—Sp	30 cm	Sow successively for continuous harvesting.
winter savory (*S. montana*)	WP. Low, straggly bush. Also in prostrate form.	Cuttings—Sp and A Layering—Sp	40 cm	Cut back after flowering.
Sweet cicely (*Myrrhis odorata*)	HP. Soft, green, fernlike stems growing to 80 cm.	Seed—A Division—A	50 cm	Slow to germinate.
Tansy (*Tanacetum vulgare*)	HP. Dark green, vigorous, spreading clump, grows to 90 cm. Can rampage.	Division—Sp and A	70 cm	Very hardy. Keep under strict control. Good compost plant.
Tarragon French tarragon (*Artemisia dracunculus*)	HP. Bright green, spreading plant, grows to 40 cm.	Division—Sp	30 cm	Dig and replant every 2–3 years. Needs frost protection.
Thyme (*Thymus vulgaris*)	WP. Dark green, aromatic, compact bush growing to 30 cm.	Seed—Sp Layering—Sp, S and A Division—Sp	30 cm	Good low hedge or border plant. Trim after flowering.
caraway thyme (*T. herba barona*)	WP. Green, spreading ground cover, grows to 5 cm.	As for thyme	30 cm	Good ground cover for dry areas.
lemon thyme (*T. citriodorus*)	P. Green, spreading shrub, grows to 20 cm.	As for thyme	30 cm	Silver and gold varieties. Good for rockeries and borders.

Herb	Habit	Propagation	Spacing	Comments
orange thyme (*T. fragrantissimum*)	P. Blue-grey, straggly, spreading bush. Grows to 30 cm.	Seed—Sp Cuttings—Sp and A	20 cm	Keep trimmed.
wild thyme (*T. serpyllum*)	P. Matting ground cover growing from 3–20 cm high.	Seed—Sp Division—Sp and A	30 cm	Excellent hardy ground cover and lawn plant.
Valerian (*Valeriana officinalis*)	P. Tolerant, spreading, light green clump, grows to 1 m or more.	Seed—Sp Division—Sp and A	60 cm	Lovely back of border plant. Flowers in second year.
Vervain (*Verbena officinalis*)	P. Dark green, leafy clump, grows to 80 cm. Dies back in W.	Seed—Sp (erratic germination)	30 cm	Old cultivar. Cut back in W.
Weld (*Reseda luteola*)	B. Low rosette in 1st year. Flowering spikes to 1 m in 2nd year.	Seed—Sp	50 cm	A dyer's plant. Good back of border plant.
Woad (*Isatis tinctoria*)	B. Blue-green clump in 1st year. Flowering stalk to 1 m in 2nd year.	Seed—Sp	50 cm	Unusual flat, black, papery pods. A dyer's plant. Good back of border plant.
Woodruff (*Galium odoratum*)	P. Spreading, bright green plant growing to 30 cm.	Seed—LS Division—S	20 cm	Germination may take 12 months. Will not grow in hot, dry conditions.
Yarrow (*Achillea millefolium*)	P. Low, spreading, feathery, green clump with flowers to 1 m.	Seed—Sp Division—Sp and A	50 cm	Can be invasive. Good ground cover in wild areas.
sneezewort (*A. ptarmica*)	P. Spreading, leafy clump with flowering stems to 50 cm.	As for yarrow	30 cm	Ornamental and easy to grow.

INDEX

The page numbers in **bold** type indicate illustrations.

Agrimony 23, 26, 29
Alpine strawberry 28
angelica 21, 26
Anise 26, **27**, 29
Anise hyssop 26, 27, 29
anthemis 28
applemint 29
artemisias 21, 26, 28
aureum feverfew 28
    marjoram 28
balm 14
Balm of Gilead 26, 27, 29
Basil 14, **15,** 26, 28, 29
    leaves 34
Bergamot **16,** 16, 26, 27, 29
betony 21, 27, 29
borage 13, 27, 29
bronze fennel 28
bugle 21, 28, 29
calendula 26, 29
camphor 26, 28
caraway 26, 27, 29
catmint 21, 26, 27, 28, 29
catnip 27
chamomile 26, 28, 29, **34**
    flowers 34
chervil 21, 26
chives 21, 26, 28, 29
clary sage 28
Cloches 13
Comfrey 15, 21, 23, 29, 33
common sage 28
coriander 13, 26, 29
Corsican mint 28

costmary 16, 21, 26, 28
    leaves 34
cotyledons 13
Curry plant 14, 21, 27, 28, 29
Cuttings 14
digitalis **23**
Dill 13, 26, 29, 33
dwarf lavenders 28
dwarf rosemary 28
dyer's chamomile 29
elecampane 23, 29
Evening primrose 10, 21, **26,** 26, 29
fennel 13, 21, 26, 29
    Foeniculum vulgare
feverfew 21, 28, 29
Foxgloves 21, **23**
French tarragon 14
garlic 28
    chives 29
Germination 13
golden marjoram 29
ground ivy 21, 28
Harvesting 35
Height 29
Herbs for Dry Ground 19
Herbs for Shady Places 21
Herbs for Watery Surrounds 23
horehound 21
hypericum 21, 29
hyssop 14, 21, 27, 28, 29
Improving Drainage 10
lady's bedstraw 16, 21, 26, 28, 29
Lady's mantle 21, 29
Lavender **7,** 14, **20,** 21, 26, 27, 28, 29

Lawn chamomile   28
Layering   17
lemon balm   16, **18,** 21, 26, 27, 29
    grass   26
    verbena   14, 26
lovage   26, 29
lungwort   27, 29
    valerian   21
mallow   10, 21, 26
marjorams   21, 26, 27, 28
marshmallow   21, 23
meadow clary   21
meadowsweet   21, 23, 26, 28, 29
mignonette   26, 27
Mint   14, **14,** 16, 21, 28, **32**
motherwort   27, 29
mugwort   21
Mulching   10
mullein   21, 28, 29
musk mallow   21, 29
Nasturtiums   **19,** 21, 28, 29
Oregano   26, **27,** 28
orris   21, 29
Parsley   **11,** 12, 13, 21, 28
pennyroyal   **17,** 21, 28
peppermint   **23**
perennial chamomile   21
Picking   35
pineapple sage   29
Preparing the Soil   10
Preserving   36
prostrate rosemary   28
    winter savory   28
purple basil   28
Pyrethrum   26, 28, 34
red sage   28, 29
red yarrow   29
rocket   21, 26
Roman chamomile   29
Root Cuttings   15

Division   16
Rosemary   14, 15, **16,** 21, 26, 27, 28, 29
rue   14, 21, 26, 28, 29
Sage   14, 15, **16,** 17, 21, 26, 27, 28, 29
salad burnet   21, 28
santolina   14, 21, 27, 28, 29
savory   21, 27, 28
Scent   26
seed-growing mix   12
sneezewort   23
soapwort   23, 29
Sorrel   **9**
summer savory   29
Sweet bay   26, 28
Sweet cicely   21, 23, 27, 29
Sweet marjoram   **21,** 29
sweet violet   21
sweet woodruff   28
Tansy   21, 27, 28, 29, 33
tarragon   27
Thyme   **17,** 17, 27, 28
Tropaeolum majus   **19**
valerian   23, 26, 29
vervain   21
violets   28
wall germander   21, 28
wallflower   21
weld   21, 29
Welsh comfrey   29
white horehound   28
wild strawberry   21
wild thymes   28
winter savory   14, 29
woad   29
wood sage   21
woodruff   21, 29
woolly thyme   28
Wormwood leaves   34
Yarrow   16, 21, **28,** 33, 29